BRITAIN IN OLD PHOTOGRAPHS

LOUGHBOROUGH

DAVID R. BURTON

The
History
Press

Left: Loughborough Grammar School from Leicester Road, *c.* 1900.

Title page photograph: Loughborough Town Hall, *c.* 1992. The clock had been silent for some sixteen years, after people complained that the chimes disturbed their sleep. Charnwood councillors were looking into proposals to allow the chimes during the day.

First published 1997
This edition published 2009
Reprinted 2019

The History Press
97 St George's Place, Cheltenham,
Gloucestershire, GL50 3QB
www.thehistorypress.co.uk

British Library Cataloguing in Publication Data.
A catalogue record for this book is available from the British Library.

ISBN 978 0 7524 4978 4

Typesetting and origination by The History Press
Printed in Great Britain by TJ International Ltd. Padstow. Cornwall.

CONTENTS

Market day outside the Town Hall, 9 September 1910. The Lord Nelson inn is in the distance. Boots Cash Chemist published the postcard and this one was sent to someone in Blackpool.

INTRODUCTION

Loughborough in Old Photographs is my fourth book in this series. I have enjoyed compiling all of them. The three previous books are about Leicester, where I was born in 1935 and grew up, but I have also had – and still have – family connections with Loughborough. The photographs in this book are mostly from the archives of the *Loughborough Monitor* and *Leicester Mercury* and thus they are of first-class quality. Also included are pictures from my own collection of postcards and family photos, as well as those of friends. Many of these photographs would not have seen the light of day if not presented here.

Books such as this are full of nostalgia. In today's busy world memories are often a tonic, especially when they evoke happy times. Of course, not all our recollections are happy ones.

I make no apologies for errors: the information in the captions was given to me in good faith (and any mistakes will be rectified in future editions). Thank you for reading *Loughborough in Old Photographs*, and I hope you enjoy it.

David R. Burton

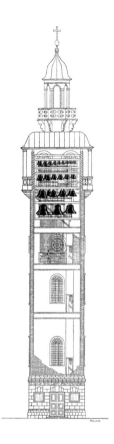

The Carillon was opened on 22 July 1923, and stands 153 ft high. This memorial to the dead of the First World War is one of Loughborough's best-known landmarks. It contains forty-seven bells weighing almost 21 tons: 'toll for the brave, the brave that are no more'.

Queen's Park, c. 1920. Crossing the rustic bridge is a young man in blazer and boater; the scene is very typical of the 1920s.

ONE

AROUND THE STREETS

The cross marks 2 Toothill Road, the home of the sender of this postcard, c. 1913.

Devonshire Square, *c.* 1968. A lot can happen in thirty years and people forget very easily. The market-place is on the left.

The top of the market-place, *c.* 1988. Older residents will remember the James Vaults inn, which used to stand where Boots is now; the inn disappeared in the fifties. On the left was the Nelson inn.

A fine aerial view of Loughborough, to the south of the town centre, *c.* 1967. Shelthorpe Road is at the bottom of the picture.

Baxtergate, *c.* 1981. This is the shape of things to come with alterations to kerb lines and the planting of trees. In the early 1900s the street was much narrower. The Rose and Crown, dating from Victorian times, was a popular inn in Baxtergate.

Loughborough town centre, *c.* 1968. Swan Street is on the left and Churchgate on the right. In the 1950s shops in Swan Street included Coleman's outfitters, Mr Kirke's confectioners, W.H. Smith and Curry's.

High Street, *c.* 1924. Stanley Day's clothes shop is on the left, and the Bull's Head Hotel sign is prominently placed across the road. This Robin Hood postcard published by C. and A.G. Lewis Ltd of Nottingham was sent by Elsie to her mother in Yorkshire.

The market-place, *c.* 1927. The two chemists' shops of Martin and Latimer stood almost side by side. The range of buildings from Hepworth's on the left to Martin's was built in the early 1700s. Mr Stain the printer, Mr Aslett the chemist and Mr Jones, who succeeded him, all used to live above the shop. Now it's all gone.

High Street, *c.* 1900. Notice the gas lamps outside the shop premises, and the cyclists and horse-drawn vehicles.

Swan Street, *c.* 1908. Again, notice the large gas lamps outside the premises on the left, the cobbled road and the striped sun awnings on the shops.

The view along Leicester Road, looking towards the town centre from no. 229, *c.* 1985. The shops may have changed but the roof lines are the same.

Leicester Road, *c.* 1920. In those days cyclists were a long way off the ground! Chamberlains' motor garage was on the left, with the Home Café next door.

Ashby Road, *c.* 1985. This was once described as the most elegant length of road in Loughborough.

Baxtergate at night, just before Christmas, 1983. The shops are full of gifts, the windows ablaze with lights.

The view along Market Street towards the Town Hall, 1990. It is August and the town is full of shoppers and visitors.

Shakespeare Street, c. 1983. Most corner shops like this one have disappeared from many towns today.

The corner of Pinfold Gate and Leicester Road, *c.* 1983. The scene is so quiet it must have been a Sunday.

Bedford Square, *c.* 1983. The cars confirm the age of this fine *Leicester Mercury* photograph. In the 1950s Bramleys' fruit shop was one of the best-known shops in the square. On the left is the Wheatsheaf Hotel; at this time Mr James was the licensee.

New pedestrian signs were a part of the first phase of a three-part plan to give Loughborough town centre a face-lift. The first phase was finished by around 1988. Work was planned to pave the market-place.

The view along Pinfold Gate towards the A6, c. 1982. Artisans Cottage on the right was empty but the building was saved from demolition by conservationists. The cottage was built in the nineteenth century to house employees of the Cotton Hosiery Machine Co.

Churchgate, which leads to the parish church, viewed from Biggin Street junction, *c.* 1979.

Loughborough market-place, with the Lord Nelson inn in the centre, *c.* 1968.

High Street, *c.* 1923. The overhead sign advertises the Bull's Head Hotel Commercial and Posting House. Loughborough Rotary Club, which held its meetings there, was founded at this time.

Forest Road, *c.* 1930. Houses like these were typical of Leicestershire at this date.

Churchgate modernised, *c.* 1988. Managers Joe Elsegood and Geoff Sulley were both colleagues of the author, and worked at Whitchers (seen on the left) in Leicester, Hinckley and Stroud.

SECTION TWO

BUILDINGS

All Saints' Church, Loughborough. The chancel was constructed in the thirteenth century and the nave in the fourteenth. The fifteenth century saw the construction of the clerestory and the nave roof. The tower was built at the west end in the sixteenth century. In the seventeenth century the church was used as a garrison, stable and prison in the Civil War. Galleries for musicians were erected in the eighteenth century. An appeal in the nineteenth century saved the church but the work continues.

This tinted postcard of Loughborough Town Hall was printed in Germany, *c.* 1900. The Town Hall, built in 1855, was a popular subject for postcard publishers.

Charles Lowe & Sons' premises at the Great House in Churchgate. The furniture company was established on this site over a century ago.

Woodgate Baptist Church on Southfield Road, *c.* 1970. Demolition had started only a few days before this picture was taken.

Loughborough's Memorial Baths, *c.* 1971. Once the town's pride and joy, they were built in honour of the dead of the First World War.

An imposing view of All Saints' parish church from the front gates, *c.* 1988. (See also page 21.)

The interior of Loughborough's ancient parish church, *c.* 1967. The new cross replaced the earlier more traditional one.

Interior view of All Saints' parish church, 1920. This postcard was published by Boots.

Loughborough Rectory, *c.* 1970. This photograph appeared in the *Loughborough Monitor* newspaper.

Burleigh Fields House in Radmoor Road, Loughborough, *c.* 1973. This building dates back to the early 1800s.

Burleigh Fields House, *c.* 1976.

Loughborough's second (and last) workhouse, built in 1838 and seen here in about 1977. This was the administration block, and the wards were on either side. The Derby Road entrance had two archways with gates. The conditions for the inmates were poor and the discipline harsh. In 1977 it became Hastings House, an old people's home.

The imposing entrance to Loughborough police station, *c.* 1955.

'Hatches, matches and despatches': this is the Register Office in Ashby Road where 200 couples tied the knot in 1969. The Children's Department had recently moved to modern premises.

An old corner of Loughborough disappears to make way for the new precinct, c. 1971. This site was formerly occupied by the Green Man pub, Grudgings' sweet shop, Colemans the clothiers and Cluleys the butchers.

The Volunteer in
Devonshire Square, one
of Loughborough's oldest
public houses, *c.* 1979. It
was closed in 1979 and
the Trustee Savings Bank
wanted to demolish the
late eighteenth-century
building to build a new
banking hall.

Clemersons Corner,
c. 1972. Behind the
hoardings work is
in progress on the
foundations of one of
Loughborough's two new
precincts.

Interior view of the fifteenth-century Merchants House in Warners Lane, Churchgate, *c.* 1975. At one time it was occupied by the Irish Menswear shop.

All Saints' Rectory, 1930s. It is a very imposing building, and still stands today.

The old rectory, c. 1959. The Georgian front was rebuilt after a fire in 1830. The top part was added later but the lower part is medieval.

Demolition of the medieval Merchants House in Churchgate, *c.* 1975. The half-timbered construction is clearly visible.

Chesterton House in Rectory Place, *c.* 1988. Described as a fine late Georgian town house, this was one of the most splendid of Loughborough's historic buildings.

The Great Central Hotel on King Street, *c.* 1967. Work was about to begin on an extension containing thirty bedrooms and a new cocktail bar. The manager at the time was Mr Ronald Elliott.

The ancient Manor House in Sparrow Hill, 1983. E.L. Fisher's shop on the left sold plumbing and electrical goods; on the right was B. Jones the ironmongers. The whole building had been sold and would later be converted into a restaurant.

Demolition of the Theatre Royal, *c.* 1972.

Demolition in progress at the Theatre Royal, *c.* 1972. Fallen timber and bricks lie where once children sat entranced through Saturday matinées. The owner, Mr Charles Deeming, ran the theatre from the mid-1930s to 1953 when, like so many other theatres, it was forced to close. When the building was declared unsafe, Charles Deeming ordered it to be demolished. Entertainers including Roy Castle, Norman Wisdom and Hylda Baker all appeared here.

The new Imperial Buildings were unveiled to a mixed reception in 1980. One person even described them as looking like a public lavatory. The original Imperial Buildings were built in 1928 by the Jackson family.

Old High Street, *c.* 1920. Stanley Day's shop is on the right.

The Railway Inn in the Rushes, later known as the Charnwood, *c.* 1930. Until 1883 it was The Plough and the licensee at that time was W.T. Swann. The name was changed when the railway line was opened from Loughborough to Coalville.

SECTION THREE

SHOPPING

Shops in Nottingham Road, c. 1980. The right half of this building was soon to be demolished and rebuilt.

Putt's shop in Sparrow Hill, *c.* 1920.

Mr J.L. Putt seated in one of Phillip Bartholomuch's ice-cream vans in the 1930s. Mr Putt was a painter and decorator who designed and painted the ice-cream vans.

Loughborough Monitor Office (now the *Leicester Mercury* news shop), *c.* 1950. The *Loughborough Monitor* was founded in 1857 by J.H. Gray, a draper turned printer. A prominent member of the Woodgate Chapel, he lived for a time at 25 Leicester Road. He published the paper from offices near Angel Yard. He died aged 40 in 1873. The *Monitor* amalgamated with the *News* in 1870. In 1880 Francis Hewitt, proprietor of the *Leicester Daily Mercury*, founded the *Loughborough Herald*. Hewitt amalgamated the *Herald* and the *Monitor and News*; in 1938 it became the *Loughborough Monitor and Herald* but the 'Herald' was later removed. Herbert W. Cook was the editor at this time. Harry Martin and Paul Grinnell are the present district reporters.

Wards End, *c.* 1969. New shops with modern frontages have appeared, but the upper buildings were unchanged.

Covered stalls in the market-place, *c.* 1905. On the right is the Lord Nelson Inn and next door is C. Dufner, watchmaker, jeweller and optician.

Clemersons' furniture retailers, *c.* 1971. This scene has changed dramatically: when Clemersons' was demolished people could see the Carillon from the market-place.

The photograph above was taken around the turn of the century on part of what was known as the Loughborough Navigation, which was originally part of the River Soar. It was opened in 1778 and connected with the River Trent. There were several sections of navigation, which were all joined up on 1 January 1932 and now form the Grand Union Canal.

One of Loughborough's longest-established businesses, this is Priestley's shoe shop in Churchgate, pictured in 1974 shortly before it was due to close. The owner was Mr D.E. Garner.

A typical Victorian shop front, *c.* 1910. Young, Pilsbury & Young's shop windows are packed with displays, set off with black and gold fascia boards.

The market-place, *c.* 1929. This is another busy day, with lots of stalls. The Latimer family seem to have cornered the market, with a jewellers, opticians and chemists in the same row of shops!

The market-place, 1970. The stalls were normally erected by council workmen, but at this time they were on strike. Stallholders had to find cover as best they could: here we see fruiterer and florist Mr Syd Powell of Sparrow Hill and his assistant Miss Susan Oram sheltering under his giant brolly.

Whitcher's Menswear, photographed from Warners Lane, c. 1994. This shop closed in October 1994. In the early 1900s it was Moody's, then Curringtons in the 1920s before Whitcher's took over in 1954. Mr Joe Elsegood worked there from 1928 and Mr Geoff Sulley, the last manager, worked there from 1967 until the shop closed.

A view of the roof construction in a cruck cottage at the back of Whitcher's shop in Churchgate, c. 1980. This cottage dates back to 1723.

This old pump stood behind Whitcher's shop in Churchgate. The pump is dated 1723 and it is pictured here in the 1980s.

An old fireplace in the back of Whitcher's shop in Churchgate. This was the kitchen area of the cruck-built cottage. Local schoolchildren used to visit these premises on history tours.

SECTION FOUR

INDUSTRY

*John Taylor & Company's bell tower and foundry, built in
1829, pictured in 1972. The factory now stands in a very
pleasant housing development from where tree-lined walks lead
through to the town's shopping centre.*

Visitors at John Taylor's foundry, *c.* 1988. They are admiring the variety of bells on show after visiting the Taylor Museum on their conducted tour.

In 1987 Taylor's foundry received an order for thirteen bells for All Saints'
Church, Leighton Buzzard, which had been badly damaged by fire and its
bells distorted and cracked. Pictured is fitter Steven Phillips with the bells
ready for despatch. Twelve of the bells were named after the apostles.

Sileby parish church bellringers visited Taylor's foundry in 1978 to watch
the casting of two new bells for St Mary's Church. The ringers had raised
£800 in eight months to have two old bells melted down and recast. One bell
came from the chapel in Sileby Cemetery tower and the other from Sileby
Roman Catholic Church. St Mary's now has ten bells.

The Sileby bellringers watch as the craftsmen at Taylor's start the process of putting music into metal as they cast the two bells for St Mary's Church, Sileby.

This huge bell, weighing 16¾ tons, was called Great Paul, and it is shown here on its way to St Paul's Cathedral in 1882, where it remains. The journey took nearly two weeks. Two Fowler steam engines hauled the bell on a specially made trailer.

Opposite below: Fitter Charles Phillips (left), bellmaster Mike Milson and Managing Director Alan Berry (right) pictured with the new clavier, *c.* 1987. Some of the bells were bound for Florida. Charles Phillips has worked at the foundry for thirty-seven years.

The forty-seven bells in the Carillon tower, which opened on 22 July 1923. This postcard dates from around 1930. All the bells have names, and many have a verse too.

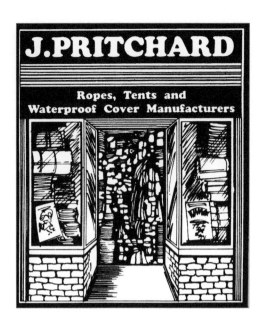

J. PRITCHARD

Ropes, Tents and
Waterproof Cover Manufacturers

This etching shows John Pritchard's shop in Swan Street. The company was first established in 1820 by Robert Pritchard, John's father. He was the principal church bell rope maker in England and his workshop was in Cumberland Road. The company traded from Swan Street until 1927 when the shop was destroyed by fire. Later that year a new workshop was established in Biggin Street, and moved to Freehold Street in 1982.

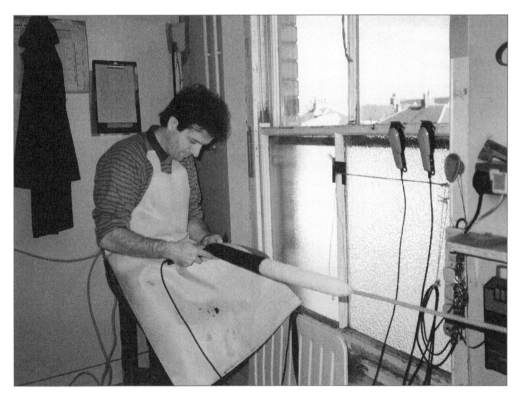

Alan Wilson trimming the sallie on a bell rope at John Pritchard's, 1988. The sallie is 100 per cent wool and is put into the rope as it is made on the rope walk. The main part of the rope is flax. Alan Wilson has been with the company since leaving school twenty-five years ago. He is the fifth generation of the Wilson family to have worked at Pritchard's.

Alan Wilson sewing a canvas awning at John Pritchard's. The firm has made marquees and awnings for over a hundred years.

David Wilson inserting the wool yarn into the twist of the bell rope to form the sallie. David Wilson has worked on the rope walk for many years.

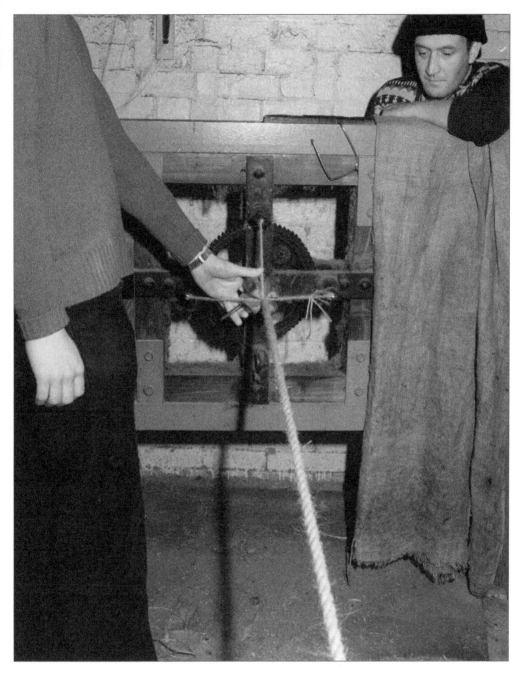

Andrew Robertson and David Wilson at the rope walk at Pritchard's. This picture shows how the twist is put into rope with the aid of a shuttle.

This is one of John Pritchard's marquees at Loughborough race course down Swingbridge Lane, pictured in 1920.

Rikers' new pharmaceutical factory, *c.* 1968. It cost half a million pounds and was opened in 1969.

Mr Derek Sharman makes the sparks fly in 1988. He is refurbishing the Town Hall clock at H. Adey & Sons' ironmongers, where he has worked for thirty-two years.

The Round House at the entrance to the Brush works on Nottingham Road, *c.* 1973, shortly before demolition. The Round House dated from the 1890s.

The Brush works, *c.* 1920. In 1865 the company was Henry Hughes & Co. but was later taken over by Falcon Engineering. This postcard was published by Hartman.

Chargehand Mr Jim Prickett, of 31 Leopold Street, Loughborough, working on a generator motor to be used on a freight locomotive, pictured at Brush Electrical, *c.* 1976.

This transformer was made by Brush Ltd over a hundred years ago.

The fire at the Brush engineering works, c. 1921. This postcard was published by W.H. Smith and Co. of 21 Baxtergate.

Type two locos being built at Brush, *c.* 1957.

This Brush type S 1 1–050 HP diesel locomotive is being loaded aboard the *Benhiant* at the Royal Albert Docks for export to the Philippines, *c.* 1969.

These two railcar-mounted gas turbine-powered generating sets, made at the Brush works in Loughborough, are pictured on their way to Montreal for shipping on to China in 1974.

Wrights Mill, in Market Street (formerly Mill Lane), *c.* 1980. Luddites smashed the machines in John Heathcoat's factory formerly on this site.

The new extension to Loughborough College, which housed the swimming pool, gym, badminton and squash courts, pictured in 1938.

Loughborough College New Block at the corner of Frederick Street and Packe Street, *c.* 1936.

LOUGHBOROUGH COLLEGE.
Department of Automobile Engineering.-
Internal Combustion Engines Laboratory.

Loughborough College Department of Automobile Engineering and Internal Combustion Engines Laboratory, *c.* 1930.

Mr John Martin snr (right) with John Martin jnr (left) and Paul Martin, pictured at Loughborough Crane Hire in Mill Lane, *c.* 1975.

The new Sainsbury's site on the corner of Ashby Road and Greenclose Lane, looking very drab on a wet day in 1978.

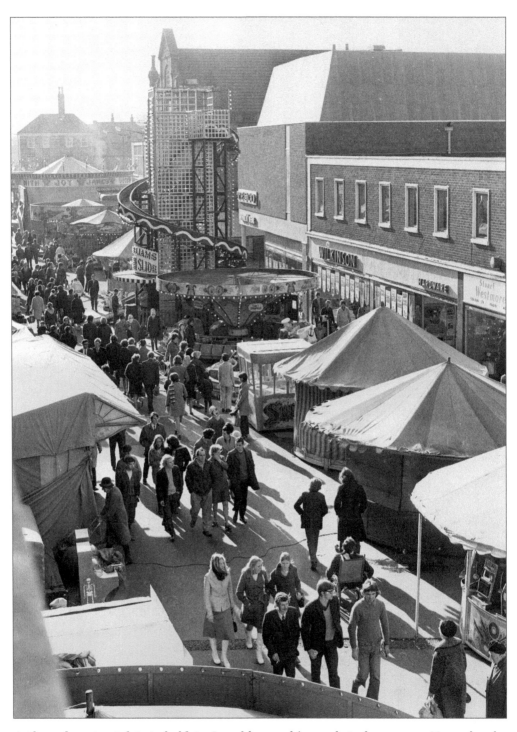

A three-day street fair is held in Loughborough's market-place every November by permission of a charter signed by King Henry III in 1228. In 1970 the fair was opened by deputy mayor, the Revd J.N.L. Thompson.

SECTION FIVE

PEOPLE

Employees of Brush Switchgear, Loughborough, and their friends, pictured in 1981.
They are about to set off on their carnival bicycle ride from Loughborough to Leicester
to raise funds for handicapped children at Stretton Hall Hospital, Great Glen.

One of the projects for the six- and seven-year-olds of Fairfield School, Loughborough, was to assemble a collection of Victoriana. Aided by their grandparents they gathered stone hot water bottles and teddy bears. Here Abigail Dickinson (seated), Jenny John and Richard MacKay look at a picture which Jenny's 86-year-old great-grandmother had acquired by collecting labels from sardine tins.

A busy town centre scene in Churchgate, 1984. The area was newly pedestrianised.

Charnwood Mayor, Councillor Reg Burton, accompanied by his wife Olive, opens 79 King Street after refurbishment. Also present are Mr Ken Higgs, Councillor Michael Brayshaw, Mr Malcolm Miller and Councillor Jim Walker.

The Mayor of Loughborough, Revd J.N.L. Thompson, viewing a scale model of the town centre redevelopment, *c.* 1969. With the Mayor are Mr E. Davis (left) and Mr W. Davis, the contractors.

Gala Day at Fearon Hall school, *c.* 1982. Mr Mervyn Walters welcomes the Mayor of Charnwood, Councillor Ernest Shardlow, and the Mayoress, Councillor Mrs Marion Simpson. They were accompanied by members of the fund-raising committee at the new community centre.

The presentation of an English bone china plate, decorated with four well-known Loughborough scenes painted by Mr Derek Walsam of Queniborough, 1983. Present are the Mayor of Charnwood, Mrs Margaret Ward, Mr Arnold Ward, Mr Bruce Wheeler and Mr Derek Walsam.

The history of Britain's oldest foundry has been officially documented for the first time by the curator of Taylor's, Mr Trevor Jennings. In 1987 he handed over the first copy of his book *Master of My Art* to Mrs Merle Taylor, the widow of Paul Taylor who was the last member of the original family.

The Mayor of Burnaby in British Columbia visited Loughborough in 1984 to pay tribute to the man from whom his town took its name. Robert Burnaby emigrated to Canada from Leicestershire in the 1850s, returning fifteen years later and settling in the hamlet of Woodthorpe. Pictured are Mr W. Lewarne, Mayor of Burnaby, his wife Mrs J. Lewarne, Mr Reg Burton, Mayor of Charnwood, Mrs Olive Burton and Canon Michael Banks, the rector.

Working at Brush is a family tradition for the Hardy family. Father Mr Maurice Hardy trained the managing director and production director when they were apprentices. Mark Hardy, Maurice's son, is now on the way up with his father's help.

Aggrieved allotment holders on the Ingle Pingle site, which the council intended to close, *c.* 1983. Left to right: Mr Vernon Bentley, Mr Charles Boucher, Mr Leonard Sharpe, Mr R.G. Kirby.

Halfway between the industrial estate and Loughborough's sewage works lay an overgrown field which was home to nine caravans in 1971. The families living there were waiting to be rehoused by the council. One resident at that time was Mrs Sheila Cloherty.

The Revd David Paterson, vicar of St Peter's Church, spent nine hours on the roof of his church to collect donations to church funds in 1979. In this picture, coffee is on the way up to him in a bucket. Also present are Hilda and Mabel Barber.

Canon Michael Banks, rector of Emmanuel Church, looks on as Councillor Bill Lewarne and his wife from Burnaby in Canada lay a wreath on the grave of Robert Burnaby, founder of his Canadian town, in 1984. Also pictured are Councillor Reg Burton and his wife Olive, the Mayor and Mayoress of Charnwood.

Mr Paul Taylor (left) with a party of bellringers from Sileby Church in 1978. They are looking at a bell wheel while waiting for the temperature to be right for casting. Left to right: Paul Taylor, G.C. Lane (churchwarden), Wilf Preston of Sileby parish council, Tom Dexter (the oldest ringer), Jim Dexter, Stuart Crick (ringers), Jim Healy (churchwarden), Edna Preston.

In 1982 the managing director of Brush Electrical Machines, Mr Bill Creswick, presented First Aid certificates to twenty-four employees. These are some of the successful candidates. Front row, left to right: Mr K. Smith, Mrs S. Tomlin, Mr A.R. Creswick, Mrs J. Gamble, Mr E. Price, Mr G. Abell, Mr W. Holland (Works First Aid Officer). Back row: Mr W. Moir, Mr D. Bunker, Mr R. Owen, Mr N. Burton, Mr T. Rae, Mr C. Butler, Mr M. Barsby, Mr S. Boyes.

In 1976 gold watches were presented to forty-six long-serving Brush employees, four of them to women members of staff. They are, from left to right, Mrs E. Tebbutt, Mrs D.L. Bright, Mrs M. Purday and Mrs F. Webb, and they are pictured with Mr J.M. Durber.

Mr T.W.B. Sallitt, the managing director of Brush Transformers Ltd, explains a feature of a Brush transformer to Mr L. Kadoorie, chairman of the China Light and Power Company, Kowloon, Hong Kong, who visited the works in 1971. Also in the picture is Mr C.W. Pass, the managing director of Hawker Siddeley Electric Export Ltd.

The presentation of a cheque to Harry Dukes of Brush Transformers on his retirement in 1976. Harry had previously worked in a Teesside shipyard, joining Brush in 1964. Left to right: Maurice Dukes, George Turner, Mr D. Hickling, Harry Dukes, Bill Hind, George Dukes.

In 1982 Roy Ballantyne, chairman and managing director of Brush Transformers Ltd, presented long-service awards to employees. They are, from left to right, Royston Barker, Ron Grice, Mr R. Ballantyne, Reg Stewart, David Sharp, David Fisher, Mrs Freda Kendall, Norman Cox and Stan Boneham.

Members of Baxtergate Baptist Church dressed up in period costumes to celebrate their jubilee 1828–1978.

Edgar and Florence Woods on holiday on the east coast (probably Hunstanton) with their daughters Margaret, Kathleen and Dorothy.

Kathleen, Dorothy and Margaret Woods of Albert Promenade, *c.* 1935. Their mother was a dressmaker.

Edgar Woods in his Pay Corps uniform, 1916. At this time he was stationed at Sheerness. Originally from Donnington in Lincolnshire, he was manager of the Home and Colonial in the market-place until 1939 when he moved to Leicester to start his own business. He married Miss Florence Powell of South Witham in 1920.

Mr and Mrs Culpepper Valpy with Kathleen Woods (centre) in the garden of their home in Lime Avenue, c. 1940.

Kathleen and Dorothy Woods with their cousins Ron Woods and Alma Burton, *c.* 1929.

Kathleen, Dorothy and Margaret Woods outside 66 Albert Promenade, Loughborough, *c.* 1931.

Schoolgirls Kathleen and Dorothy Woods
in their Loughborough High School
uniforms,
c. 1938.

Kathleen and Dorothy Woods in their
Sunday best in the doorway of 66
Albert Promenade, *c.* 1938.

Margaret Woods at the wheel of a pedal
car in 1936. Now living in Solihull, she
is still driving.

Dorothy Woods poses for the
photographer in the garden of 66
Albert Promenade, *c.* 1938.

SECTION SIX

LEISURE

Feeding the ducks in Queen's Park, 1985. In the centre is the Carillon which is played at 1 p.m. on Thursdays. There are recitals too during the summer.

Mr Eddie Preston the gardener raking up the leaves in Queen's Park in 1984. It was a mammoth task but well worthwhile, adding to the pleasure of visitors to the park.

Sydney Potter, the Deputy Carillonneur, at the keyboard in the Carillon, 1925.

The entrance to Queen's Park, looking towards the Carillon, *c.* 1940.

A quiet corner in Queen's Park, 1984. Time to relax and enjoy the open air.

Brookside Walk in Forest Road, *c.* 1971. There are now plans to extend this walk to the Outwoods.

The flats by the canal, one of the winners in the Charnwood design awards competition, 1984.

Big Meadow, *c.* 1992. This has been owned by local families since 1760 and is home to a variety of rare beetles and wild flowers.

Winter in Queen's Park, February 1969. The Carnegie Library in the background was opened in 1905 by former Mayor Joseph Griggs.

Queen's Park bandstand, 1993. Built for the Silver Jubilee of Queen Victoria, it is still used for concerts during the summer.

Knightthorpe Park, 1978. The stream which runs through the park brings back joyful memories of jam jars, fishing nets, minnows and sticklebacks to many people who grew up in Loughborough.

An icy morning in Queen's Park, 1985. The Carillon stands aloof over the park.

This gardener's cottage in the tree-shrouded garden formerly belonged to Stensons Breweries of King Edward Road. It is pictured in around 1971. The head of the company was Alderman Fred Stenson.

Peter Waller, Paul Brailsford and Kevin Rose pose beside the wall they helped to build at the Outwoods, *c.* 1985.

The end of the Ash Grove in 1989. The three ash trees stood at the south-western corner of Charnwood Water, where the town's famous family of brickmakers, the Tuckers, dug out the clay, creating a large hole which filled with water; it was known locally as 'Tuckers Claypit'.

The old railway line along which steam locomotives travelled between Loughborough's Derby Road LNW station and Coalville. It now provides a pleasant tree-lined walk, and is pictured here in 1978.

This photograph, taken from the balcony on the Carillon tower in Queen's Park in 1969, shows the line of the new road linking Wards End and Frederick Street.

SECTION SEVEN

EDUCATION

Loughborough Grammar School's chemistry laboratory, c. 1900.

A wooden tractor made by pupils at the De Lisle School in Loughborough in 1977. Left to right: Paul Clamp, Martin Billson, Paul Davie.

Pupils at St Mary's School, Loughborough, receive their prizes, 1980. The headmistress, Sister Mary David, has been a teacher for forty years and head at St Mary's for twenty-five years. She joined the Rosminian Order during the Second World War and taught at Shepshed, Earl Shilton and the Isle of Wight. Pictured with Sister Mary David are Lisa Calladine, Richard Kogut, Alison Metson, Lisa Jane Oliver, Mark Dowse and Martin Dakin.

Pupils and staff of Loughborough Grammar School, *c.* 1930.

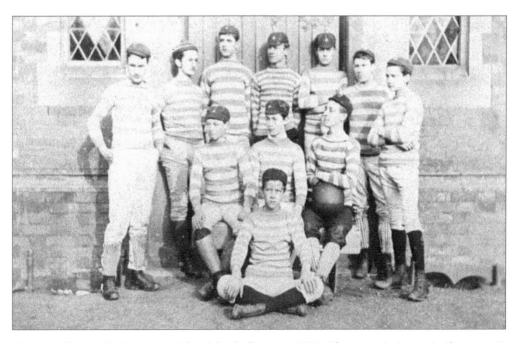

The Loughborough Grammar School football team, 1885. They are C. Scott, G. Shenton, O. Taylor, G. Oliver, W. Clarke, C. Campion, G. Carter, S. Stephenson, W. Slater, K. Hanson and S. Stevenson (captain).

Loughborough Grammar School pupils who won places to Cambridge University in 1896, photographed with members of staff.

Loughborough College students second seven-a-side team, *c.* 1976. Back row, left to right: Pat Marsh, Paul Beak, John Thornton, Jed Glynn, Kevin Douglas, Keith Trudgeon. Front row: Ray Black, Nick Cousins (captain), Hugh Preston.

Loughborough Grammar School staff, *c.* 1895. They look very strait-laced.

The presentation of scrolls at the Spriggs Memorial Lecture at Burleigh College, 1976. Left to right: Martin Sadler, Mr G.H.F. Broad, Kevin Billson and Neville Stack, editor of the *Leicester Mercury*, who presented the awards.

Mr Barry James, the local director of Barclays Bank, presents prizes for public speaking to Loughborough Girls' High School pupils. Left to right: Jennifer Turnbull, Julia Fordham and Charlotte Smith. (Photo: Barclays Bank)

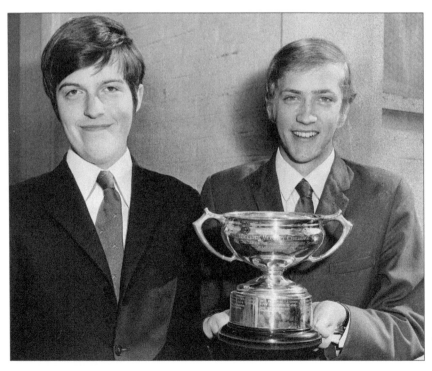

Michael James (left) and Nigel Irons of Loughborough Grammar School with the *Leicester Mercury* trophy that they won in the inter-schools debating competition in 1973.

This is the bust of a former Loughborough headmaster, Alfred Thomas Eggington, known as 'The Boss', who died in 1982. He was also Mayor of Loughborough. The bronze bust was sculpted by Nirava Kavya of Melton Mowbray. Standing, left to right: Stan Merriman, Maurice Bray, Eric Acons, Howard Seaton, David Asher, Bert Coote. Seated are Bill Boyden (left) and Donald Hutchings.

Staff and pupils of the former Loughborough College School from the 1950s and 1960s, pictured in 1983. Left to right: Bernard Cross, Gordon Broad, Janet Butler, Des O'Leary, Sandy Campbell, Alan Dunsmore, Carol Dunsmore, Ken Harfitt, Bob McLarnon, David Knowles, Fred Modral.

Rosebery Street Junior School, Loughborough, 1929. All the children are smiling and well scrubbed for the occasion. Many of these youngsters still live in the area. Second from the left in the front row is Ken Sutton; fourth from the left is Jimmy Scattergood. Second from the right in the third row is Eric Clarke.

Mr J.A. Ferrigan with some of his pupils on the occasion of his retirement after eighteen years as headmaster at Garendon School, Loughborough. He was also a lay reader and a Rotarian.

Kenneth Harrison (headmaster) and Terry Murphy (deputy headmaster) of Loughborough's De Lisle School with some pupils viewing an award which they had won. The award was made under the Royal Society's 'Education for Capability Recognition Scheme'. Mr Murphy's project was a skills programme. The award was presented by Viscount Caldecote.

Members of Garendon School radio club demonstrate their equipment to parents at a prize-giving evening, 1969. Left to right: Neil Onions, Dale Sharp, David Brown, Peter Brown.

A new Church of England Primary School was opened in Loughborough by the Bishop of Leicester, the Rt Revd Dr Richard Rutt, in 1989. In the special dedication service he rang the bell to welcome pupils. The new building replaced the Warner and Emmanuel Schools. The head is Mrs Jan Kirkham.

Mrs Rosina Matthews with pupils from Loughborough's Cobden Primary School who had won the coveted John Rodgers Cup for Road Safety Quiz, *c.* 1979. Left to right: Sunil Patel, Susan Dowdine, Hasna Rahman, Teresa Whiteman, Alan Jones, Richard Warrington.

The two cricket teams of the Grammar School – pupils and parents – pictured before their match in 1975. Back row, left to right: M. Drone, T.P. Jones, R. Beaton, J. Heaney, J. Storer, J. Bayes, J. Marriott, H. Heaney, J. Sturgess, A. Swift, V. Inkey. Front row: N. Chappell, R. Usher, A. Stevens, A. Underwood, M. Rose (captain), P. Merriman (captain), R. Cotton, M. Meredith, G. Ledger. Front: R. Merriman and S. Jones.

Loughborough High School sports trophy winners, 1979. Back row, left to right: Emma Taylor, Joanna Caldwell, Katie Jones, Lisa Thomas, Julie Fagernes. Front row: Kathryn Stevens, Emma Lockwood, Vicky Adams, Anne Townsend.

Kenneth Harrison retired in 1981 after seventeen years as headmaster of Loughborough's De Lisle School. He was born in Morecambe. The school had grown during his headship from 390 pupils to over 1,000.

The assembly hall at Loughborough Grammar School, 1905.

A fine photograph of Loughborough Grammar School, 1991.

The grass-covered quadrangle of Loughborough Grammar School, pictured here in 1976, easily fits into the traditional image of public school architecture.

Hazlerigg Hall at Loughborough College on its opening day, *c.* 1938.

Loughborough High School, 1975.

SECTION EIGHT

TRANSPORT

Miss Joan Meakin, publicist on the paper, seen with the
Leicester Mercury *glider at Stoughton, c. 1930.*

The intrepid aviator Gustav Hamel dropped copies of the *Leicester Daily Post* at Loughborough, twelve miles away, in 1912. Six members of the newspaper staff assisted with the take-off. Hamel flew at 200 ft at a speed of 35 miles an hour.

This *Leicester Mercury* photograph from 1931 shows van driver Arthur Sleath loading papers for Skegness; they were also delivered to Loughborough. Mrs Margaret Sleath also worked for the *Mercury* from 1929 to 1936.

An evocative picture of a steam locomotive pulling into the station at Loughborough in 1984.

Locomotive no. 4 *Robert Nelson* at Loughborough central station in 1977. Pictured from the left are David Hinton, Michael Whitehouse and Harold Porter.

The last scheduled passenger train about to leave Loughborough central station for Nottingham in 1969.

Third year boys from Garendon High School, Loughborough, pictured in 1969 admiring the steam lorry belonging to Peter van Howten of Hathern, who built it from scrap in 1956. His son Peter was in the third year.

The glass coach made a spectacular wedding vehicle for Mr Howard Cole and Miss Georgina Farnham in 1969. They had known each other since they were children and attended Fairfield Kindergarten School, Loughborough.

Two cars converted into ice-cream vans by a body shop in 1930. They were painted by
J.L. Putt (see page 40). The rear entrance to Putts' premises is in the background.

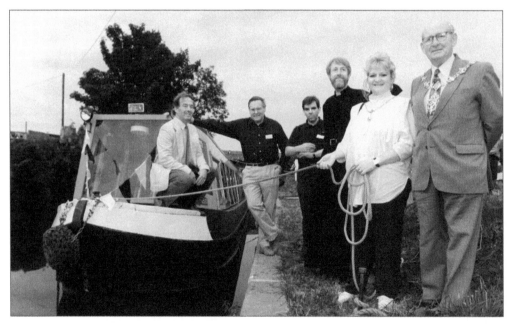

The 200th anniversary of the opening of the Leicester Navigation Canal was celebrated
in 1991. A cavalcade of boats travelled from Chain Bridge, Loughborough, to Leicester
after a thanksgiving service on the towpath, led by Revd Stephen Cherry, Rector of
Loughborough. Left to right: John Evans, Brian Williams, Stuart Holland, the Revd
Stephen Cherry, the Mayor and Mayoress of Charnwood, Councillor Gus Thornton and
Mrs Louise Cooper.

SECTION NINE

EVENTS

Her Majesty the Queen arrives at the Brockington Building at Loughborough University, followed by the Mayor and Mayoress of Charnwood, 1989.

Smiles all round as HRH Princess Diana stops to talk to members of Charnwood Mencap Society on 22 March 1984, during her visit to Glebe House.

Glebe House in Forest Road, the headquarters of the Charnwood Mencap Society, pictured in 1984.

Major-General W.T. MacFarlane inspecting the Guard of Honour at Loughborough Grammar School as he arrives to make the annual inspection of the Combined Cadet Force in 1976.

Rear Admiral Richard Hill inspecting members of the Loughborough Grammar School Combined Cadet Force in 1982; with him is the Commanding Officer, Colonel Don Wood, who has been with the CCF since 1957.

A parade by the Loughborough Grammar School Combined Cadet Force in 1975. The inspecting officer is Group Captain D.J. Green, officer commanding RAF Swinderby. The cadets' CO is Colonel D. Wood.

Unveiling the restored fountain in the market-place, 1981. Left to right: David Tarver (sculptor), Peter Beecham, John Todd (Borough Surveyor), the Mayor of Charnwood, Councillor Frank McKeown, and the Mayoress, Mrs Nora McKeown.

Miss D.E. Andrews, the retired head of Loughborough High School, plants a tree to mark the opening of Loughborough's Fairfield School's new buildings in 1969. Left to right: Miss D.E. Andrews, Mr H.W.A. Lewis, Miss D.M. Jefferies, Miss P.J. Hadley (Miss Andrews' successor). Mr Lewis and Miss Jefferies were joint heads of the school.

Some of the twenty-nine courageous pupils of Ashmount special needs school in Loughborough showing off their awards for learning to swim under the Penguin scheme in 1984.

A major gas leak in Green Close Lane caused traffic chaos in 1995; Sainsbury's store and other premises nearby all had to be closed.

Troops on parade in Loughborough market-place for their homecoming, 1919. The postcard was printed by Smith & Co., Kodak Stores, Baxtergate.

The United Reformed Church in Frederick Street, 1910. The banner reads 'God Bless Our Sailor King'.

ACKNOWLEDGEMENTS

Many people have helped me to compile this book and without them I could not have succeeded. Special thanks to my wife Beryl for her help and patience, my son Stuart and his wife Annie for typing and computer skills. To Steve England and his staff in the Library at the *Leicester Mercury*. Also my thanks to Steve Martin, David Putt, Herbert Putt, Ross Nimmo, Geoff Sulley, Mrs D.E. Shirley, Margaret Townsend, and Kathleen Wickham who is sadly no longer with us. To Michael and Ann Potter, Margaret Portess, Jerry Caesar, and also John Slater of the Loughborough Library.

To all of them, my grateful thanks.

David R. Burton

The boat cavalcade from Loughborough
arrives at West Bridge, Leicester, 1991. The
boat, the *Duke of Bridgewater*, was loaded with
a symbolic cargo of coal.

Other titles published by The History Press

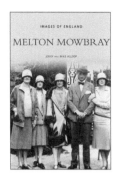

Melton Mowbray

JENNY ALLSOP

A collection of approximately 200 archive images accompanied by captions, offering a look at the history of Melton Mowbray, taking the reader on a journey around the streets and buildings, recalling people and events which have shaped the character of the town.

978-0-7524-3774-3

Haunted Leicester

ANDREW JAMES WRIGHT

This creepy collection explores the supernatural side of Leicester and its surrounding area, seeking out spectres and phantoms and recounting their tales. From the cathedral and opera house to pubs and streets, this journey around Leicester's spooky spots will enthral those interested in the city's haunted heritage.

978-0-7524-3746-0

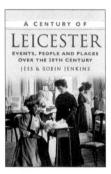

A Century of Leicester

ROBIN JENKINS

A Century of Leicester offers an insight into the daily lives of local people and gives glimpses and details of familiar places during a century of unprecedented change. Many aspects of Leicester's recent history are covered, famous occasions and individuals are remembered and the impact of national and international events is witnessed. It also celebrates the character and energy of local people as they move through the first years of this new century.

978-0-7509-4918-7

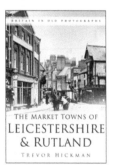

The Market Towns of Leicestershire and Rutland

TREVOR HICKMAN

Trevor Hickman's new book draws on his unsurpassed collection of prints, engravings and photographs to capture bygone days in the nine market towns of his home county of Leicestershire. Leicester (before 1919, when it officially became a city), Market Harborough, Melton Mowbray, Loughborough, Lutterworth, Hinckley, Ashby de la Zouch, Oakham and Uppingham are all included; and we explore their distinctive histories in the company of the county's foremost local historian.

978-0-7509-4137-2

Visit our website and discover thousands of other History Press books.

www.thehistorypress.co.uk